Tiptoe Into Scary Places

FRIGHTENING FARMS

by Rachel Rose

Consultant: Debbie Felton
Professor of Classics
University of Massachusetts
Amherst, Massachusetts

BEARPORT PUBLISHING

Minneapolis, Minnesota

Credits

Cover, © Kim Jones, © DianeDugas-Imagen.com/Shutterstock, © Robyn Mackenzie/Shutterstock, © flashbacknyc/Shutterstock, and © Chris Bradshaw/Shutterstock; 3, © Arden Jordan/Shutterstock; 4-5, © Kim Jones, © Kenneth Keifer/Shutterstock, © Dennis W Donohue/Shutterstock.com, and © Harry Adam/Shutterstock.com; 6, Wikimedia Commons/Public Domain; 7, © Valery Sidelnykov/Shutterstock and © Scorpion_PL /iStock; 8, © AF Archive/Alamy stock photo; 9, © 3DMI/Shutterstock and © vesna cvorovic/Shutterstock; 10 , Wikimedia Commons/Public Domain; 11, © Haywiremedia/Shutterstock, © Grigorita Ko/Shutterstock, and © Happy monkey/Shutterstock; 12, © n_defender/Shutterstock; 13, © Bob Bell/DrivingBackroads.com; 15, © Flyby Photography/Alamy Stock Photo; 16, Wikimedia Commons/geograph.org.uk; 17, © Eric Ehrlich/Shutterstock and © John Gomez/Shutterstock; 18L, Wikimedia Commons/Public Domain; 18R, Wikimedia Commons/Public Domain; 19, Bidgee/Wikimedia Commons; 21, © Karen Culp/Shutterstock, © Julia Shepeleva/Shutterstock, and © Everett Collection/Shutterstock; 23, © David Steele/Shutterstock; and 24, © volkovslava/Shutterstock.

President: Jen Jenson
Director of Product Development: Spencer Brinker
Editor: Allison Juda
Designer: Micah Edel
Cover: Kim Jones

Library of Congress Cataloging-in-Publication Data

Names: Rose, Rachel, 1968– author.
Title: Frightening farms / by Rachel Rose.
Description: Minneapolis : Bearport Publishing Company, [2021] | Series: Tiptoe into scary places | Includes bibliographical references and index.
Identifiers: LCCN 2020002572 (print) | LCCN 2020002573 (ebook) | ISBN 9781647471736 (library binding) | ISBN 9781647471798 (ebook)
Subjects: LCSH: Haunted farms—Juvenile literature. | Ghosts—Juvenile literature.
Classification: LCC BF1477.2 .R67 2021 (print) | LCC BF1477.2 (ebook) | DDC 133.1/22—dc23
LC record available at https://lccn.loc.gov/2020002572
LC ebook record available at https://lccn.loc.gov/2020002573

For more information, write to Bearport Publishing, 5357 Penn Avenue South, Minneapolis, MN 55419. Printed in the United States of America.

CONTENTS

FRIGHTENING FARMS

It is the dead of night. You are lying in bed inside an **eerie** farmhouse. You begin to hear a knocking sound. It seems to be coming from inside the walls! You pull the blankets over your head. But wait—what's that tugging at your hair?

Get ready to read four spooky tales about farms. Turn the page . . . if you dare!

LEAVE THE LIGHTS ON!

The Old Arnold Estate, Harrisville, Rhode Island

The Perron family moved into an old farmhouse in 1971. As the previous owners left, they warned the Perrons to keep the lights on after dark. One frightening night, they found out why.

The Old Arnold Estate

They were **jolted** awake by the ghostly figure of an old woman shouting. Who was this figure, and why was she there?

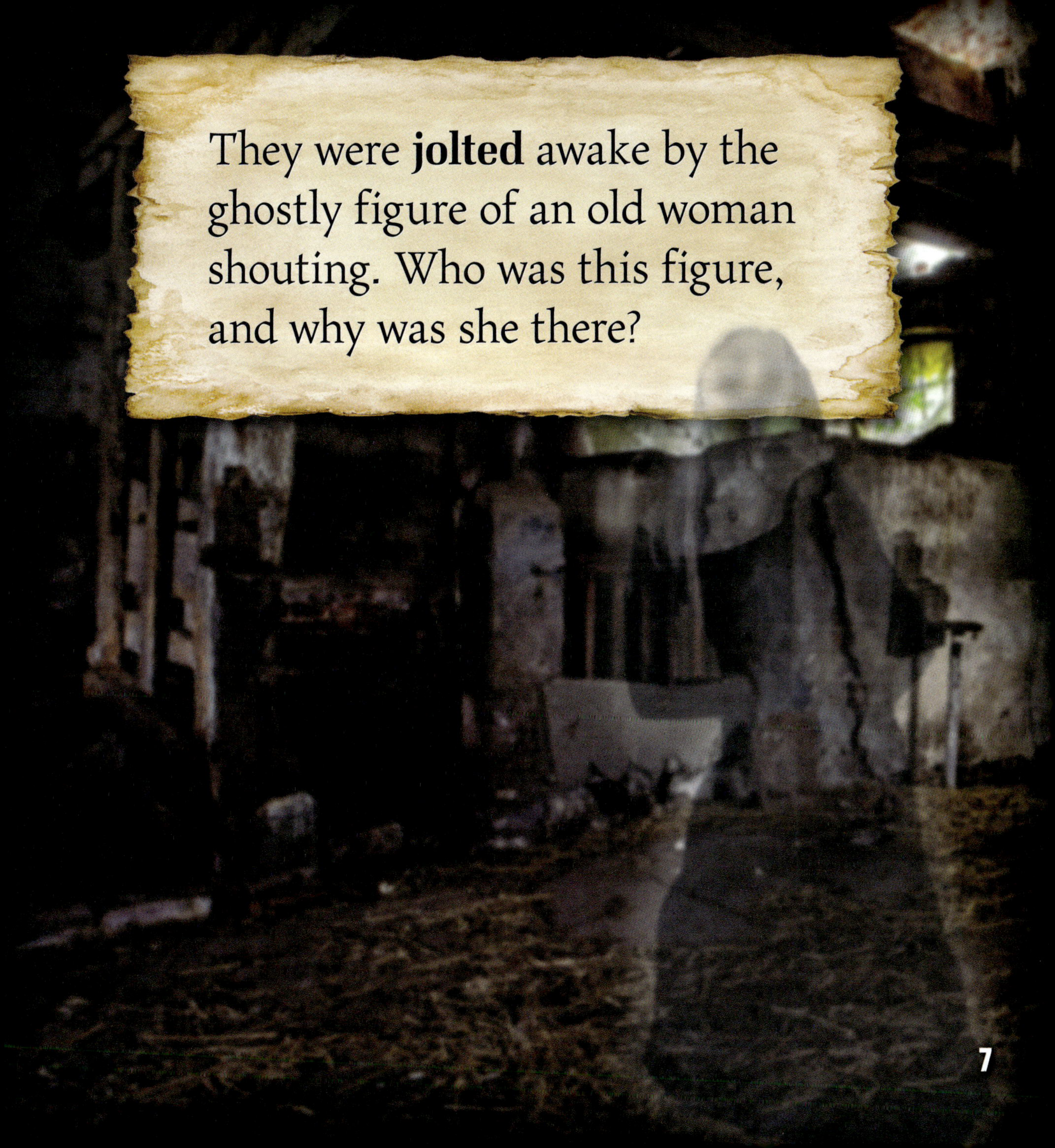

It is believed the Perrons were visited that night by the **spirit** of Bathsheba Sherman. Bathsheba was thought to be a witch who had lived in the farmhouse more than 200 years earlier.

The 2013 film *The Conjuring* was based on the **supernatural** events that happened at the Old Arnold Estate.

The Perron family kept hearing spooky voices and the sound of doors banging. They sometimes smelled foul odors like rotting flesh. The children were even smacked, pinched, and dragged across the floor!

THE CURSE OF THE BELL WITCH

The Bell Farm, Adams, Tennessee

Not long after John Bell moved his family to a farm in Tennessee in 1817, strange and spooky things began to happen. One day, John saw an **incredible** creature. It had the body of a dog and the head of a rabbit!

John Bell's old house

At night, his family heard scratching sounds and knocking inside the walls. John's daughter Betsy was pinched and poked. Yet no one was there.

Some say these strange hauntings were the work of John's neighbor, Kate Batts. Kate was thought to be a witch who put a **curse** on John and threatened to kill him. John died **mysteriously** in 1820. Today, people who visit the farm still hear strange sounds.

After John died, a small bottle filled with liquid was found near his bed. When the family gave it to the cat to drink, the cat died immediately. No one knew where the bottle came from.

Eerie Whispers

Elvey Farm, Kent, England

Elvey Farm is located in the **quaint** English village of Pluckley. Today, it is used as a small hotel. Visitors come to stay in what is said to be the most haunted village in England. Several of the village's spirits have been seen roaming the grounds at Elvey Farm. One of the more famous ghostly guests is the spirit of Edward Brett.

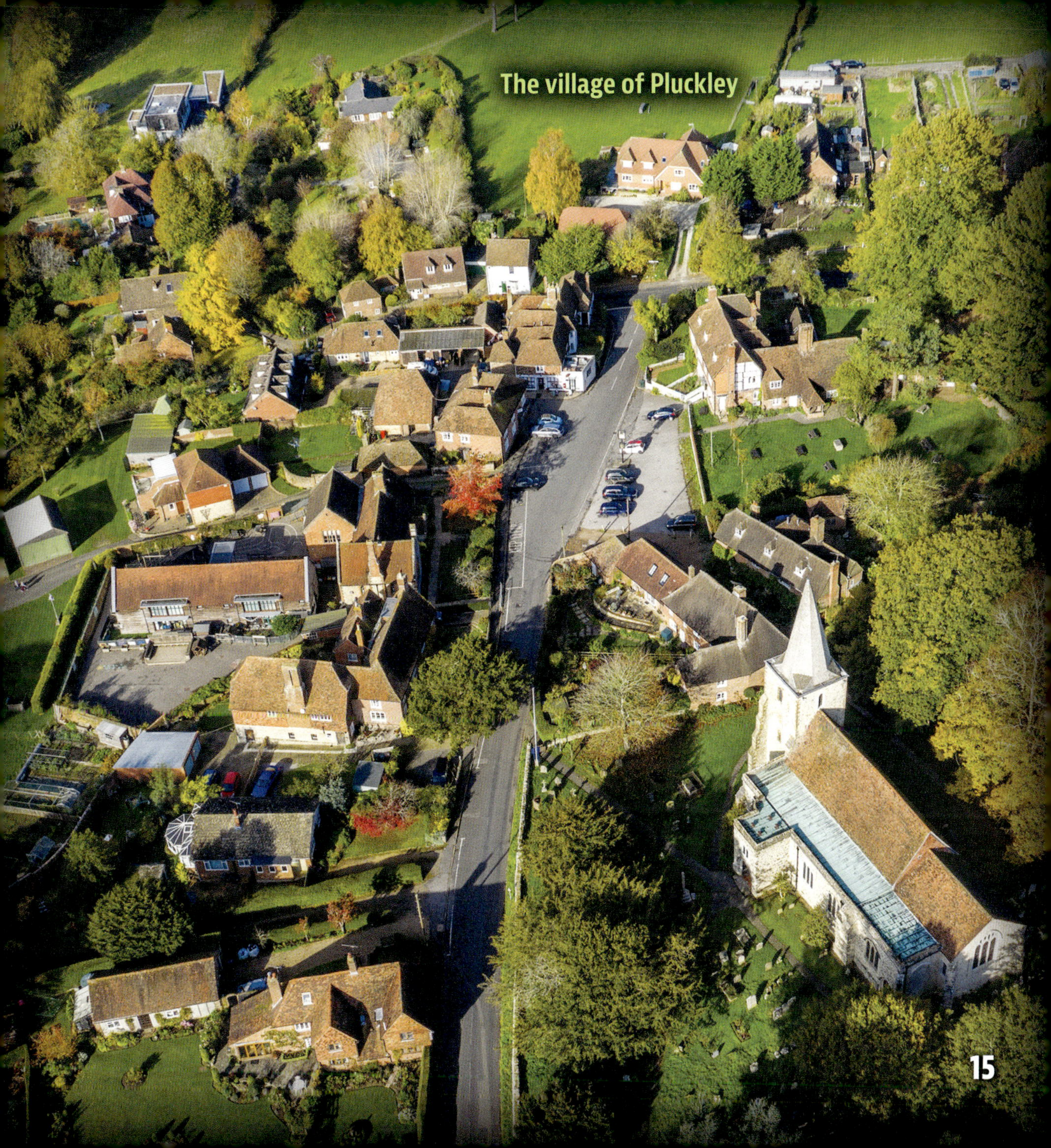
The village of Pluckley

Edward owned the farm over 100 years ago. One day, he shot himself in the dairy barn. Today, guests at the hotel report hearing the eerie whisper of Edward's ghost.

Other ghostly **presences** include the thief Robert DuBois and a man in a military uniform who appears at the top of stairs. Have these spirits also come back to whisper their secrets?

Elvey Farm

Robert DuBois would hide behind a tree and then jump out to rob his victims. One day, someone threw a knife at him, pinning him to the tree.

TRAGEDY STRIKES

Monte Cristo Homestead, New South Wales, Australia

Death—and possibly murder—followed shortly after Christopher and Elizabeth Crawley built the farmhouse of their dreams in 1884. A baby died after a nanny said an invisible force pushed it out of her hands as she stood at the top of the stairs. After that, a maid was pushed from a balcony, and a barn fire killed a boy who worked there.

Christopher and Elizabeth Crawley

Monte Cristo Homestead

After her husband passed away, Elizabeth Crawley became so sad she almost never left the house. She died there at age 92.

In 1963, Olive and Reg Ryan moved into the house. When they arrived, bright lights shone from inside even though the electricity was off. They have felt ghostly touches and heard their names whispered throughout the house.

The Ryans also say they've seen white, shadowy figures in photographs taken at the home. Could these be the ghosts of the long-dead Crawleys?

Creepy Farms Around the World

The Bell Farm
Adams, Tennessee

Visit this farm's strange creatures and hear its spooky sounds.

The Old Arnold Estate
Harrisville, Rhode Island

Meet Rhode Island's most famous witch.

Elvey Farm
Kent, England

Watch out for the ghotstly farmer and the thief.

Monte Cristo Homestead
New South Wales, Australia

Explore one of Australia's most haunted farms.

GLOSSARY

curse (KURSS) something that brings or causes evil or misfortune

eerie (IHR-ee) mysterious or strange

incredible (in-KRED-uh-buhl) so amazing that it is hard to believe

jolted (JOLT-id) pushed or shaken

mysteriously (mis-TIHR-ee-us-lee) in a way that is hard to explain or understand

presences (PREZ-uhns) spirits felt to be nearby

quaint (KWAYNT) cute and old-fashioned

spirit (SPIHR-it) a supernatural creature, such as a ghost

supernatural (soo-pur-NACH-ur-uhl) something unusual that breaks the laws of nature

INDEX

READ MORE

Giannini, Alex. *Frightening Farmhouses (Scary Places).* New York: Bearport (2019).

Rudolph, Jessica. *Ghost Houses (Tiptoe Into Scary Places).* New York: Bearport (2017).

LEARN MORE ONLINE

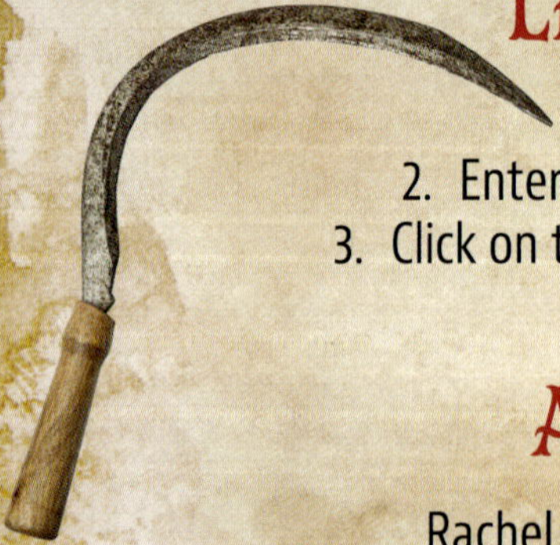

1. Go to **www.factsurfer.com**
2. Enter "**Frightening Farms**" into the search box.
3. Click on the cover of this book to see a list of websites.

ABOUT THE AUTHOR

Rachel Rose lives in San Francisco. Growing up in Ireland, she got to see plenty of farms. None of them were haunted. Or so she thought . . .